T0085638

15 ART SONGS BY BRITISH COMPOSERS

SONGS BY

BRITTEN, CLARKE, FINZI,
GURNEY, PURCELL, QUILTER,
VAUGHAN WILLIAMS, AND WARLOCK

BOOSEY & HAWKES

AN IMAGEM COMPANY

DISTRIBUTED BY

HAL•LEONARD®
CORPORATION

7777 W. BLUEMOUND RD. P.O. BOX 13819 MILWAUKEE, WI 53213

For all works contained herein:
Unauthorized copying, arranging, adapting, recording, Internet posting, public performance, or other distribution of the
printed or recorded music in this publication is an infringement of copyright.
Infringers are liable under the law.

www.boosey.com
www.halleonard.com

CONTENTS

Page

**Piano Accompaniment
CD Track No.**

BENJAMIN BRITTEN

3	Come you not from Newcastle?[1]	1
6	Nocturne[2]	2
10	The Nurse's Song[2]	3

REBECCA CLARKE

| 24 | Down by the salley gardens[2] | 7 |

GERALD FINZI

| 14 | Come away, come away, death[2] | 4 |
| 18 | Oh fair to see[2] | 5 |

IVOR GURNEY

| 20 | Sleep[2] | 6 |

HENRY PURCELL
(realizations by Benjamin Britten)

| 27 | I attempt from love's sickness to fly[2] | 8 |
| 30 | If music be the food of love[2] | 9 |

ROGER QUILTER

36	Love's Philosophy[2]	11
33	Now sleeps the crimson petal[2]	10
41	Weep you no more[2]	12

RALPH VAUGHAN WILLIAMS

| 44 | Linden Lea[2] | 13 |
| 48 | The Vagabond[2] | 14 |

PETER WARLOCK

| 54 | Take, O take those lips away[2] | 15 |

**Pianists on the CD: Richard Walters[1]
Laura Ward[2]**

Come you not from Newcastle?

Hullah's Song Book (English)

from *Folksong Arrangements Volume 3: British Isles*

original key

Arranged by
BENJAMIN BRITTEN

© Copyright 1947 by Boosey & Co. Ltd.
Copyright for all countries
All rights reserved

should — I — not speed af - ter him, since love to all is free?

Come you not from New - cas - tle? _____

Come you not there a - way? _____ O — met you not my

true love, _____ rid - ing on a bon - ny bay? _____

Nocturne

from *On This Island*

original key

W.H. AUDEN

BENJAMIN BRITTEN

WINTHROP ROGERS EDITION
Copyright 1938 by Boosey & Co. Ltd. Copyright Renewed.
All rights reserved

Now the rag - ged va - grants creep _____ In - to

crook - ed holes _ to sleep: Just and un - just, worst and

best, _____ Change _ their plac - es as _ they rest: Awk - ward lov - ers lie in

fields _____ Where dis - dain - ful beau - ty yields:

May 5, 1937

The Nurse's Song

from *A Charm of Lullabies*

original key: a minor 3rd lower

JOHN PHILIP   BENJAMIN BRITTEN

In accompaniment recording, the first vocal note is played two times before the entrance.

© Copyright 1949 by Boosey & Co. Ltd.

New transposition © 2011 by Boosey & Hawkes Music Publishers Ltd.

Copyright for all countries. All rights reserved.

this to de-sire____ I will not de-lay me. This to de-sire____ I

will not de-lay me.

più dim.

pp *senza misura*

Lull - a-by-ba-by lull-a-by-la-by ba - by, Thy nurse will tend thee as

du - ly as may be. Lull-a-by-la-by-la-by-la-by ba - by.

dim. e rit.

[Dec. 1947-Aldeburgh]

For Ralph Vaughan Williams on his birthday, Oct. 12th, 1942

Come away, come away, death

from *Let Us Garlands Bring,* Op. 18

original key: a minor 3rd lower

WILLIAM SHAKESPEARE

GERALD FINZI

© Copyright 1942 by Boosey & Co. Ltd.
New transposition © Copyright 2008 by Boosey & Hawkes Music Publishers Ltd
Copyright for all countries.
All rights reserved.

Oh fair to see

from *Oh fair to see*

original key

CHRISTINA ROSSETTI

GERALD FINZI

© 1966 by Boosey & Co. Ltd.
Copyright for all countries.
All rights reserved.

1929
[1' 5]

To Emmy Hunt

Sleep

from *Five Elizabethan Songs*

original key: B♭ minor

JOHN FLETCHER

IVOR GURNEY

© Copyright 1920 by Winthrop Rogers Ltd.

fan - cies;＿＿＿＿ that＿from thence I may feel＿＿＿ an

in - flu - ence＿＿ All＿ my powers of care be - reav - ing!＿

Down by the salley gardens

original key: E minor

W.B. YEATS

REBECCA CLARKE

Flowingly, in folk-song style

Down by the sal - ley gar - dens my love and I did meet; She passed the sal - ley gar - dens with lit - tle snow - white feet. She

In accompaniment recording, the first vocal note is played two times before the entrance.

© Copyright 1924 by Winthrop Rogers Ltd.
New transposition © 2011 by Boosey & Hawkes Music Publishers Ltd.
Words used by kind permission

I attempt from love's sickness to fly

original key

JOHN DRYDEN
and ROBERT HOWARD

HENRY PURCELL
realized by
BENJAMIN BRITTEN

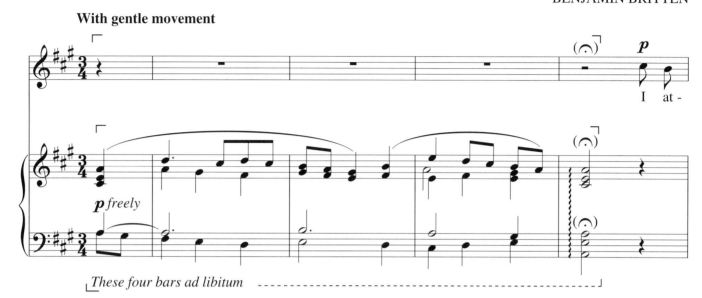

© 1960 by Boosey & Co, Ltd
All rights reserved

17

mf

No more now, no more now, fond __ heart with pride no more swell, Thou

marked

22

canst not __ raise __ forc - es, thou canst not __ raise __ forc - es, e - nough to re - bel.

warm

28

p

I at - tempt from love's __ sick - ness to fly _____ in __ vain, Since

33

I am my - self my own fe - ver, since I am my - self my own fe - ver __ and __ pain.

If music be the food of love

(1st Version)

original key

HENRY HEVENINGHAM

HENRY PURCELL
realized by
BENJAMIN BRITTEN

In accompaniment recording, the first chord is played before the entrance.

© Copyright 1948 by Boosey & Co, Ltd
All rights reserved

To Mrs. E.P. Balmain

Now sleeps the crimson petal

from Three Songs, Op. 3

original key: E-flat Major

ALFRED TENNYSON

ROGER QUILTER

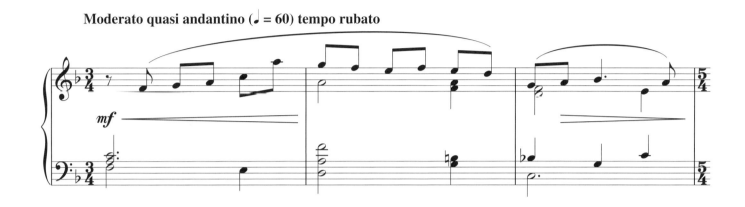

Now sleeps the crim - son pe - tal, now the white; _____

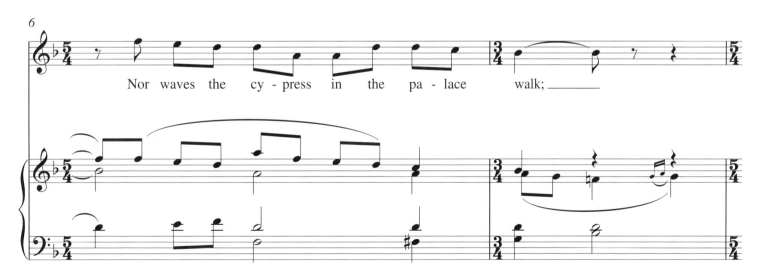

Nor waves the cy - press in the pa - lace walk; _____

Copyright © 2011 by Boosey & Hawkes, Inc.
Copyright for all countries. All rights reserved.

And slips in-to the bo-som of the lake; _____

So fold thy-self, my dear-est, thou, and slip,

In-to my bo-som and be lost, _____ be

lost in me. _____

To Gervase Elwes

Love's Philosophy

from Three Songs, Op. 3

original key

PERCY B. SHELLEY

ROGER QUILTER

Molto allegro con moto (♩ = 112)

Copyright © 2011 by Boosey & Hawkes, Inc.
Copyright for all countries. All rights reserved.

To the memory of my friend, Mrs. Cary-Elwes

Weep you no more

from *Seven Elizabethan Lyrics*

original key

ANONYMOUS

ROGER QUILTER

Weep you no more, sad foun - tains; What

need you flow so fast? Look how the snow - y moun - tains Heav'n's

sun doth gent - ly waste! But my Sun's heav'n-ly eyes View not your

Copyright © 1908 by Boosey & Co. Ltd. Copyright Renewed.

To Mrs. Edmund Fisher

Linden Lea
A Dorset Song

WILLIAM BARNES

original key: a major 2nd lower

RALPH VAUGHAN WILLIAMS

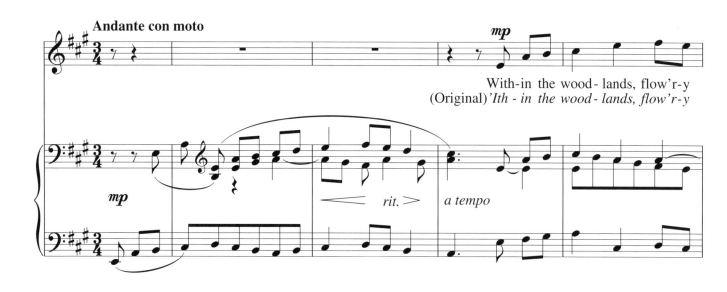

With-in the wood- lands, flow'r-y
(Original) *'Ith - in the wood- lands, flow'r-y*

glad - ed, By the oak trees' moss - y moot; The shin-ing grass blades, tim-ber shad - ed, Now do
glëad - ed, By the woak trees' moss - y moot, The sheen-en grass blëades, tim-ber shëad - ed, Now do

quiv-er un - der foot; And birds do whis - tle o - ver-head, And wa-ter's bub - bling in its
quiv-er un - der voot; An' birds do whis - sle au-ver-head, An' wa-ter's bub - blen in its

© Copyright 1921 by Boosey & Co. Renewed 1939.
New transposition © 2006 by Boosey & Hawkes Music Publishers Ltd.
Copyright for all countries. All rights reserved.

bed; And there for me, The ap-ple tree Do lean down low in Lin - den Lea
bed; An' there vor me, The ap-ple tree Do lean down low in Lin - den Lea.

When leaves, that late - ly were a-spring - ing, Now do
When leaves, that lëate - ly were a-spring - en, Now do

fade with - in the copse, And paint-ed birds do hush their sing - ing, Up up -
fade 'ith - in the copse, An' paint-ed birds do hush their zing - en, Up up -

mas - ter, Though no man may heed my frowns. I be free to go a-
meäs - ter, Though noo man may heed my frowns. I be free to go a-

broad, Or take a - gain my home - ward road, To where, for me, The ap - ple
brode, Or take a - geän my hwome-ward road, To where, vor me, The ap - ple

tree Do lean down low in Lin - den Lea. _____
tree Do lean down low in Lin - den Lea. _____

The Vagabond

from *Songs of Travel*

original key: a Major 3rd lower

R. L. STEVENSON

RALPH VAUGHAN WILLIAMS

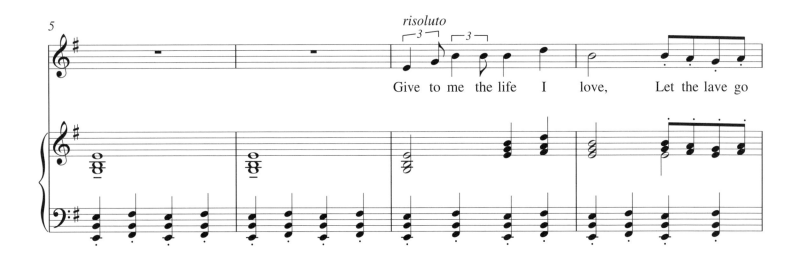

© Copyright 1905 by Boosey & Co. Ltd.
Copyright renewed 1933 in U.S.A. by Boosey & Co. Ltd.
All rights reserved.

o'er me; Give the face of earth a - round, And the road be - fore me.

Wealth I seek not, hope nor love, Nor a ___ friend to know

me; All I seek, the heaven a - bove, ___ And the

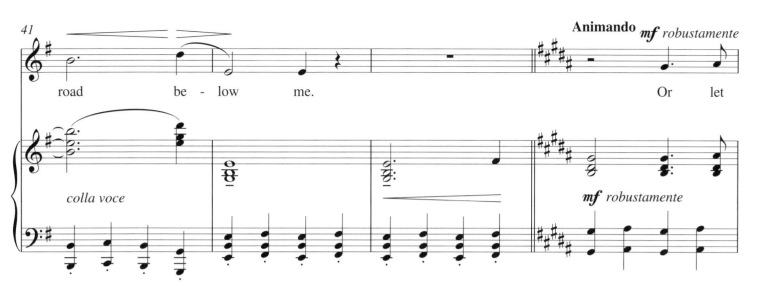

Take, O take those lips away

original key

WILLIAM SHAKESPEARE

PETER WARLOCK

Copyright 1919 by Winthrop Rogers Ltd.
All rights reserved

About the Enhanced CD

In addition to piano accompaniments playable on both your CD player and computer, this enhanced CD also includes tempo and pitch adjustment software for computer use only. This software, known as the Amazing Slow Downer, was originally created for use in pop music to allow singers and players the freedom to independently adjust both tempo and pitch elements. Because we believe there may be valuable educational use for these features in classical and theatre music, we have included this software as a tool for both the teacher and student. For quick and easy installation instructions of this software please see below.

In recording a piano accompaniment we necessarily must choose one tempo. Our choice of tempo, phrasing, ritardandos, and dynamics is carefully considered. But by the nature of recording, it is only one choice. Similar to our choice of tempo, much thought and research has gone into our choice of key for each song.

However, we encourage you to explore your own interpretive ideas, which may differ from our recordings. This new software feature allows you to adjust the tempo up and down without affecting the pitch. Likewise, the Amazing Slow Downer allows you to shift pitch up and down without affecting the tempo. We recommend that these new tempo and pitch adjustment features be used with care and insight. Ideally, you will be using these recorded accompaniments and the Amazing Slow Downer for practice only.

The audio quality may be somewhat compromised when played through the Amazing Slow Downer. This compromise in quality will not be a factor in playing the CD audio track on a normal CD player or through another audio computer program.

INSTALLATION FROM DOWNLOAD:

For Windows (XP, Vista or 7):
1. Download and save the .zip file to your hard drive.
2. Extract the .zip file.
3. Open the "ASD Lite" folder.
4. Double-click "setup.exe" to run the installer and follow the on-screen instructions.

For Macintosh (OSX 10.4 and up):
1. Download and save the .dmg file to your hard drive.
2. Double-click the .dmg file to mount the "ASD Lite" volume.
3. Double-click the "ASD Lite" volume to see its contents.
4. Drag the "ASD Lite" application into the Application folder.

INSTALLATION FROM CD:

For Windows (XP, Vista or 7):
1. Load the CD-ROM into your CD-ROM drive.
2. Open your CD-ROM drive. You should see a folder named "Amazing Slow Downer." If you only see a list of tracks, you are looking at the audio portion of the disk and most likely do not have a multi-session capable CD-ROM.
3. Open the "Amazing Slow Downer" folder.
4. Double-click "setup.exe" to install the software from the CD-ROM to your hard disk. Follow the on-screen instructions to complete installation.
5. Go to "Start," "Programs" and find the "Amazing Slow Downer Lite" application. Note: To guarantee access to the CD-ROM drive, the user should be logged in as the "Administrator."

For Macintosh (OSX 10.4 or higher):
1. Load the CD-ROM into your CD-ROM drive.
2. Double-click on the data portion of the CD-ROM (which will have the Hal Leonard icon in red and be named as the book).
3. Open the "Amazing OS X" folder.
4. Double-click the "ASD Lite" application icon to run the software from the CD-ROM, or copy this file to your hard drive and run it from there.

MINIMUM SOFTWARE REQUIREMENTS:

For Windows (XP, Vista or 7):
Pentium Processor: Windows XP, Vista, or 7; 8 MB Application RAM; 8x Multi-Session CD-ROM drive

For Macintosh (OS X 10.4 or higher):
Power Macintosh or Intel Processor; Mac OS X 10.4 or higher; MB Application RAM; 8x Multi-Session CD-ROM drive